BUDGET YOUR WAY
TO COMFORT

BEGINNERS GUIDE TO SAVING
AND INVESTING FOR YOUR FUTURE

LUKE BRANDT

authorHOUSE®

AuthorHouse™
1663 Liberty Drive
Bloomington, IN 47403
www.authorhouse.com
Phone: 1 (800) 839-8640

Published by AuthorHouse 05/14/2016

ISBN: 978-1-5246-0854-5 (sc)
ISBN: 978-1-5246-0852-1 (hc)
ISBN: 978-1-5246-0853-8 (e)

Library of Congress Control Number: 2016907683

Legal Disclaimer

This book is designed to provide information on saving and investing. The information is not a substitute for professional advice. This book should serve as a general guide. Before making any financial decisions, you should contact a professional. The contents contained in this book are based on the author's own life experiences and views. The author and associated contributors accept no responsibility for any errors and/or accuracy of information that may change over time. The author and contributors accept no responsibility for any monetary losses that may occur by readers. Saving and investing results may vary with skill level. This material is sold with the understanding that the author is not suitable to offer legal, accounting or other professional services. Therefore, no guarantees are made.

Contents

Preface

THIS BOOK IS NOT written for someone to become a millionaire overnight, but to show you how to budget and preserve some of your hard earned money through saving and investing in different avenues. This is for the average person that can never seem to get ahead, or for the working class living paycheck to paycheck wondering how to save extra money. At the end of the week, they're paying for gas with change that they dug out of there coin bank just to get to work to get their next paycheck. It always seems like it's easy for a millionaire to tell you how to save your money. But until they walk the long hard road of paying for gas or food with the change they found around the house, they really don't know what it's like.

It's a shame that nobody ever sits down and says "Look this is how you budget and save money". It has taken me years to find ways to budget, save, and invest. I learned the hard way... I started off living in a 2 bedroom 1 bathroom single wide mobile home with my wife, who was expecting. With a child on the way, we already seemed like we were struggling to pay the simplest bills and falling behind quickly. Why, you may ask...because, we were never taught how to budget and save money. We spent money on things that we wanted rather than needed. A crucial step is realizing when to separate your wants from your needs.

As you go through this book, I will prepare you to be a more cautious spender. By the end, you will have some very good tips to make you more confident and less worrisome on how you're going to live comfortably. I'm going to provide you with the basic tools to invest and to know some of the language of an investor. It's funny, before I started investing, my friend Charlie brought a one ounce silver bar into work and said "do you know what this is"? I took it out of his hand and said…"no, what is it"? He laughed and said "that's a one ounce bar of silver", I was hooked.

After investing in precious metals for some time, I wanted to learn about how to invest in the stock market. As I started learning it seemed overwhelming at first. I had so many questions I wanted an answer for and had to turn to different people to find them. At times, it felt stressful not knowing, if you were making the right investment decision.

I'm going to try to help you bypass these overwhelming feelings and teach you the basics of investing into precious metals and into the stock market. So, you don't have to feel the same stressors I did.

Acknowledgement

I'M PROVIDING THE INFORMATION throughout this book, because I am passionate about helping improve your life and help you prevent the struggles that I had to overcome. I have to first start off by giving thanks to God for providing me with the gift of this knowledge that I'm able to share with you. I also would like to thank my family and friends that supported me as I wrote this book and helped me with knowledge as I started investing. I would like to thank my wife Shannan that always is supportive of my ideas that I come up with, like writing this very book. This was something that I never thought of doing. When I came up with this idea how to share my knowledge through a book, she was very supportive (even all the time I spent away working on the book). I would also like to thank my children, as we talked at dinner during the writing of this book. We would be having a conversation about something and they would say "did you put that into your book"? They gave me some great thought going into some of the parts of the book.

I would like to thank my friend Charlie that gave me insight into precious metals and kept me interested in learning more about investing. I want to thank longtime family friend Neil for giving me insight on precious metals and the stock market when I started investing. Anytime I was looking for answers, when it came to investing, Neil was the person I turned to for sound advice. I would like to give a shout out to my friend Alan. We invested together for some time, giving each other different ideas to think about while investing. When telling him I was going to write a book, he said "that was a pretty cool idea" and very supportive.

Also want to thank longtime supporters of everything I have done over my life, my parents Kim and Darryl and my grandparents Fred and Nancy, as they all supported me through all the bumps in the road that I have encountered and helped me overcome numerous obstacles. When I told my parents I was going to write this book, they said "okay let me know when it's done" with a sound of certainty that it would be a very informational book. I would also like to thank the person that was a huge part of my childhood and we did everything together, my little sister Lauren. I also want to thank my book publisher Author House Publishing that helped me along the way with all the advice, as I was working on this book that I have created. There are so many other family members and friends that helped me along the way that I would like to thank, you all know who you are…thank you.

Basic Budgeting Fundamentals

BEFORE YOU CAN THINK about saving money and investing, you first have to break down your financials, and find how much money you're making, and how much money you need to pay your bills. When you're calculating your budget, you have to make sure you're writing everything down that you possibly spend your money on. I suggest you keep all your bill payments and all receipts that show what you spend weekly/monthly. This is going to be the easiest way to perfect your budget. I look how much my essential bills cost... your electric, water, sewer, trash, heat, cable, phone, insurance, car payment, mortgage/rent and any other bills that you pay. The only thing I exclude from this calculation is the gas that goes in your vehicle and the food that goes in your cupboard/fridge. The example provided will show you the breakdown using simple numbers. You will have to plug your numbers in to the chart to begin your breakdown.

Table 1 = Monthly Bill Cost

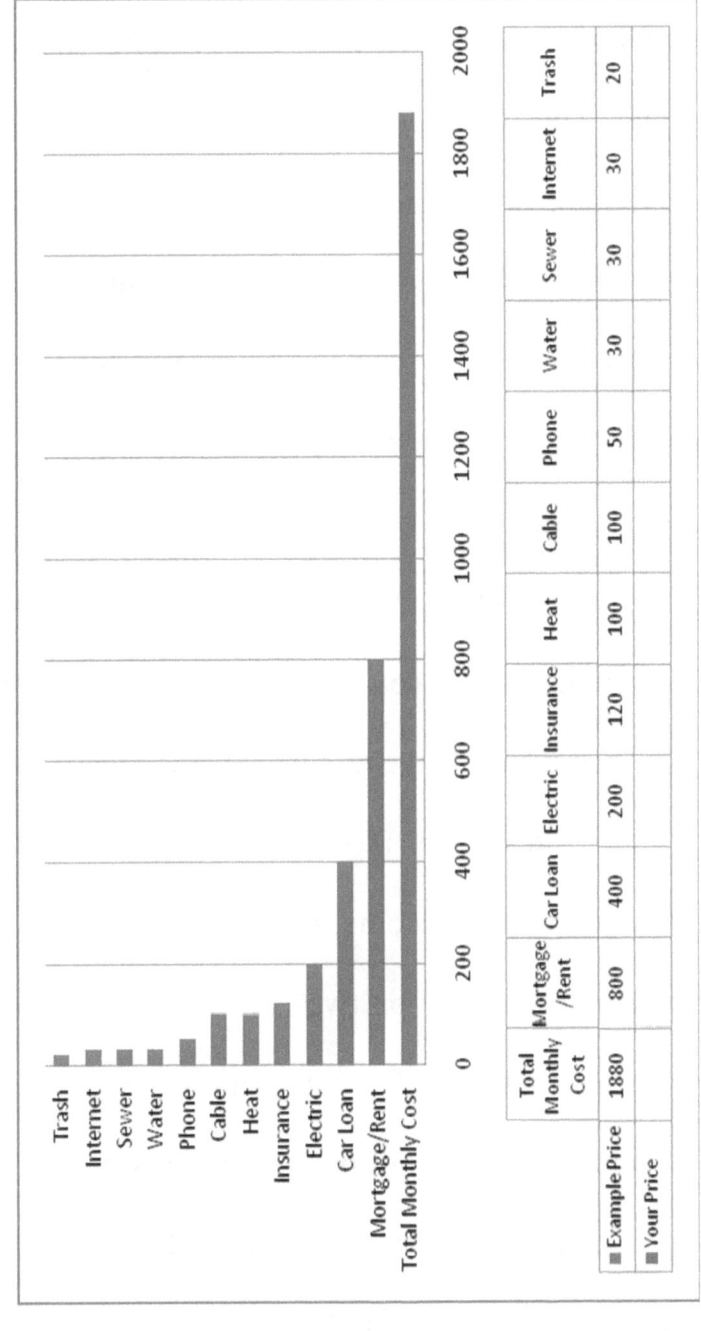

	Total Monthly Cost	Mortgage /Rent	Car Loan	Electric	Insurance	Heat	Cable	Phone	Water	Sewer	Internet	Trash
■ Example Price	1880	800	400	200	120	100	100	50	30	30	30	20
■ Your Price												

As you can see, all the numbers lined up equal to $1880.00. After you figure out the total amount for your bills, you will then divide that between four weeks of the month. Sometimes you will have five weeks in a month, and you will feel like you can go just spend extra money. But, that is a very bad decision. You need to budget properly and save that extra money. The number in the example divided by 4 weeks will be $470.00, and that is what has to be in the bank every week you get paid to pay your essential bills. If you are saying, "Luke that number is more than what I make in a week", then there has to be some other alternative. If your essential bills are going over that amount of income, then option one is to find a better primary job, option two is find a secondary job to supplement what your first job is not paying. My theory is, "If your first job is not paying the bills, then it's time to find a better job". But if you really like what you do, then add a second job. If having a second job is still not working, then an option like finding a cheaper place to live, find a roommate, or get some of your essential bills setup on a budget plan. For example if your heat bill cost $100.00/month for only 3 months of the year maybe setting up a budget with the company to divide the total of the $300 over 12 months. This is called a budget plan, some companies will work with you on a budget, and some companies won't. You would have to contact them and find out. If you're not able to meet the income for the Essential bills, it will be very difficult to get ahead. If you can pay over that Essential amount, that's a great step in the right direction.

Once you figure out your essential bill budget, you will then move on to the second step of this process called the cash carry method, which means not always using a debit/credit card. When you pay for gas and groceries, you're going to pay with cash. This is the approach I use.

I know a lot of times when you go to the gas pump, you don't feel like running into the gas station. Especially when you have kids, and you have to get them out of the car and take them in with you. This takes extra time and feels like a lot of work, but this helps you with your spending habits. A lot of times, people have their bill money in their bank account and don't realize how much they are spending on their debit card and end up spending their bill money. You go in to the gas station and spend money on a soda, cookie, bag of chips, cigarettes, cupcakes, ice tea, lottery tickets, whatever it is... but it's a dollar here two dollars there, you do that every day during the week, and believe me you're in a whole different world of money spending. What I do is, keep enough cash in my wallet to get me through to the next paycheck; the only money you need in your wallet is to put gas in your vehicle and to buy groceries. You should also save an extra $20 just in case you forget your lunch or something comes up.

Now if you are living in a joint relationship (i.e. husband/wife or boyfriend/girlfriend) at that point in time, you are going to want to split the money that it takes to be able to put gas in your vehicles. You're going to need the money to get you through the week or, if you get paid bi-weekly, then the money needs to last you twice as long. You will need to break this down to be precise, but give yourself enough movement when the gas prices go up. Today gas is $1.84 a gallon, which is down significantly, giving my family a little extra money for the week. The price of gas can change regularly, so you will have to be aware of the money you are spending when the gas prices start to rise. After budgeting for your gas, you will then want to budget the amount of money you wish to spend on groceries weekly/bi-weekly. Keep in mind, that when you are going to the grocery store, you should be able to spend a little extra to get enough to pack your lunch. Not packing your lunch can get expensive. You could easily spend $50 to $75 dollars weekly. Depending where you live in the country, the cost of food will vary. It could cost you up to $600-800 a month. In our house, one of the biggest expenses is food. Food is an essential, and when you use the cash carry method, you know exactly how much to budget for food. If you are not under the amount budgeted, you will run out of money before your next pay. Examples to keep the food budget in order would be to research the best grocery store in the area with the best prices. Take advantage of the local discount food markets and farmers markets. Shopping at stores with a reward point system can help to keep you in budget. You do not need to buy the most expensive apple, to enjoy a good tasting apple. Sometimes you are just paying for the name brand. Meat can be a huge expense at the store. You do not need to purchase a top of the line Filet Mignon. You can just get a middle priced meat, it will taste just as good.

Couponing is a great way of saving money on items when working with your budget. My wife is a coupon queen when it comes to grocery shopping. You can look through the local newspapers/ads to find the best deals in the area. When couponing, the number one rule is, just because you have the coupon, does not mean you need to buy that item, if it is not a necessity. Be sure to write a list prior to going to the store, marking which items you have a coupon for. Using a list helps you stay on track with your budget and not buying items you do not need. Another means of saving at the grocery store is to buy generic foods. Sometimes the items that you buy name brand, tastes just as good in the generic brand. I know that some items you need, you want to buy name brand, and that is ok too. We prefer to buy name brand ketchup. Think of how much money you would save if you bought generic name foods... you would only pay $1 a box for pastas where name brands would cost you $3 or 4 dollars. Most generic foods taste no different, most are using the same ingredients. At that point, you are really only paying for the name/label. A lot of the generic foods are actually made by the same company that makes the name brand foods. If you are buying bottled water, looking at the quantity and price is a good way of cutting costs. For example, if the store is selling 30 bottles of water for $3.80 and 36 bottles for $3.99, it is a smarter choice to go with the 36 bottles for $3.99.

After you break down your essential bills, gas, and groceries, you will then see how much money you have left. If you have any money left, this will be the money that you will save. This is called the 60/20/20 split. This is the method that I use to have enough money for savings and to use for investment purposes. So after you pay your essential bills and get gas and groceries, the left over money will be split in half meaning 50% will be used as savings money and the other 50% will be broken down in the 60/20/20 split. For example, if you have $200 dollars left over you will put a $100 towards your savings money and the other $100 would go 60% towards your wants and family fun money, 20% towards precious metals (bullion) and 20% stocks, bonds, and other funds. (See breakdown below)

Example: Total left after essentials and gas and groceries are paid $200

- ✓ $200 divided by 2

- ✓ $100 for savings

- ✓ $100 left- remaining is broke down in the 60/20/20 split

- ✓ 60% of $100 = $60.00 towards wants and family fun money

✓ 20% of $100= $20.00 towards precious metals

✓ 20% of $100= $20.00 towards stocks and bonds and other funds

Even though you are trying to save money and live comfortably, you need to have some fun times in your life, or you will feel like you're working just to pay bills, and that is no fun. Your 60 % fund can be used to go out as a family. You may say…"When I get a $100.00 we are going to go bowling". If there has been something that you have wanted to buy, it would come from this fund. Never buy something just because you have this extra money. Whenever I want to purchase something, I wait about a week before I go and buy it. That way, if it is an impulse buy, in a week this will pass. If you wait a week, and still want this item then go buy it. I find it is a good idea to set goals and celebrate with a day of fun or to purchase that item you have been wanting. It may take several weeks to get some money saved up to do this.

The best place to keep your emergency savings is in a savings account or a money market account. Savings accounts and money market accounts are very similar, but have some slight differences. Both will accumulate interest on your money. Usually the money market rate is a little better than a traditional savings account. Most money market accounts require a minimum balance to open the account. Some money market accounts will pay you more interest as you accumulate more money in the account. Some money market accounts will offer checks and a debit card as well, and will let you treat it like a checking account. Most savings accounts will not offer this and have a lower interest rate. It is always good to have some money on hand at your house, but I would not keep too much in your house. In the case something would happen like needing to replace a crucial household item or any type of car repairs you would use the emergency cash fund.

The second part of the 20% split is putting money towards investing into precious metals that would include gold, silver, platinum, palladium, and rhodium. There are numerous ways to purchase precious metals, and I will discuss this further in the book. The last 20% will go to stocks, bonds and other funds. This percentage will differ, if you also invest in your 401k through your employer, this will also be explained in further detail later in the book. I will also explain how I choose my stocks. When starting this approach, you may not have enough money left over to invest in precious metals or stocks right away, but having money for the emergency savings funds is a great start to get ahead in life.

For me, it took a while to reach this equation, but when using a budget you will need to realize what a want is and what a need is. You may have to sacrifice some of your wants. For example, if you see that you have extra data left over at the end of the month on your cell phone plan, lowering your plan can save you an easy $20 dollars a month. Or, if there is a better deal at another company, look into the benefits of switching. Cable is another example of cutting costs. Do you really need every movie/sports channel known to man? You can save money on your electric by just simply changing your light bulbs to energy efficient bulbs and unplugging items, when not in use. Sunlight can help with your heating bill, by opening up your blinds/curtains and letting the sunlight warm your house, preventing your heat from continual use. I found this cost cutting method by my good friend Charlie. He told me in the 70's there were no cell phones, or cable boxes which really made me think, do I really need all that I am paying for, or could I save money, if I only kept what I needed? Shopping around for deals in competing business will help to cut costs such as car insurance... also keeping a clean driving record will keep your bill low. Only putting the vehicles that you drive on your policy keeps the bill lower. If you have a bunch of extra cars you're not driving, maybe think about selling one of them. Limit your water use by taking shorter showers and keeping up on any leaks and getting them fixed, if needed.

One key point to mention is, if you have any credit card debt, this is something to really consider paying as quickly as possible. I see lots of people that have made poor choices when making purchases and living on credit cards, then can't figure out how they are going to pay the payments to the credit card companies. Credit cards are not always a bad thing and can be a great credit building tool. Using a credit card responsibly is the key, and for a lot of people this is very hard. So my general rule when using a credit card is, "if you can't pay for the item you are buying today with cash, then don't use the credit card." When you are thinking about using a credit card, you need to ask yourself, "Do I have enough money to buy this right now"? If the answer is no, then you need to save more money until the answer is yes. When you say, yes I could afford to buy this today, and you want to use the credit card as a credit building tool, then it has to be paid in full when the credit card bill arrives, so you are not paying interest. Also some credit cards can have cash back and perks to using the card, but you can't get sucked into the heavy interest credit card debt just to receive an extra ten dollars in cash back for using the credit card. The main point is: using a credit card responsibly to build credit and to save money is ok. Holding a credit balance and paying interest is not a recommended decision.

I find that sometimes, lifestyle changes need to be made with your spending habits. Sometimes addictive behaviors can affect your saving habits, such as going out every weekend partying, and running up a big bill or going gambling on a regular basis with money that should be used for your bills. These things can be a serious setback. If you find yourself in this situation, you need to look at yourself in the mirror and figure out what you need to do to improve your own situation.

In summary, I find a lot of people want things, which is a perfectly normal human instinct. But when you are chasing wants, just because other people have them is a huge mistake. You don't know how many years they saved their money for that brand new car, or if someone passed away and left them a big sum of money. You don't know what they sacrificed to get that real nice house, and you don't know how hard they worked to get what they have. I compliment people when they buy something. That might have been something they have been working towards for years. The worst thing to do is try to compete with someone that seems like they have everything. Money doesn't bring you happiness. There are professional athletes that still have problems just like the next person. Just because they have money doesn't make problems go away. So running up a credit card or going in debt just because someone else has something that you want is completely absurd! Working as hard as possible day in and day out will give you the best feeling when you do make a purchase, knowing it came from hard work.

Budget Journal

Let's figure out your budget

- Step 1) How much is your essential bills cost?____

  _____

  Answer divided by 4 weeks_____

  _____

- Step 2) how much is your weekly costs such as gas

  and groceries cost? _____

  _____

- Step 3) How much income is left after your essential bills and weekly costs are accounted for?_____

  _____

- Step 4) Take the total of step 3 and divide by 2 __

  _____

  This number will be what goes in savings____

  _____

  The other half of step 4 will be the start of your 60/20/20 split

- Step 5) what is going into your savings? _____

  _____

- Step 6) 60% of the total in step 4 will be your family fun money/ wants money _____

  _____

What is the total of fun money? _____

_____

- Step 7) 20% of the total in step 4 will be invested in
  precious metals

  What is the total invested in precious metal? _

  _____

- Step 8) 20% of the total in step 4 will be invested in
  stocks/bonds and other funds

  What is the total invested in the stock market?

  _____

  _____

Investing in Precious Metals

AFTER YOU BREAK DOWN your budget, then we can start to discuss the first 20% of savings which is used to invest in precious metals. Precious metals can also be referred to as bullion and there are several precious metals that you can invest in such as gold, silver platinum, palladium and rhodium. In this section, I will concentrate on the basics of investing in gold and silver. Gold and silver go back to biblical times as they were monetary uses, and signified value. Gold/Silver was used by many countries as currencies, however, this has dwindled down over the years when most countries stopped backing their currencies by gold/silver. Gold/silver are bought and sold globally which makes this a very good insurance policy. You probably haven't thought of this before...but, if you own any gold or silver jewelry or even silverware you already have some value. Gold/Silver jewelry are not pure. They would be too soft and easily damaged for every day wear. Pure gold is 24 karats; most jewelry is mixed with other metal alloys to make the jewelry more durable. The most common gold in North America is 14 karats. The lower the karat numbers the less gold that is contained in the jewelry. Silver jewelry and silverware also has a mixture of other metal alloys and is made up of 92.5% silver. Sterling silver jewelry will have 925 stamped on it which shows you that it has 92.5% silver. Silver and/or gold are used in many different applications such as photography, mirrors, computers, electronics and many other industry uses.

There are many different ways to purchase bullion... the physical metal which comes in many different shapes/ sizes and weights. The paper form, which means you buy an exchange traded fund (ETF), or buying a portion of a mining company that actually mines the precious metal, these will all get you exposure to the metal. Some of these can be bought on the stock exchange and will be explained later in the book. You can also buy bullion and put it in to an IRA, if it is IRA approved. There are several ways to store your bullion, a very common one is to store it in a Depository where a company will store your bullion and insure it for you. They will do routine audits to make sure your bullion is accounted for which makes it much less of a hassle than trying to find the extra space of storing it in your own home, although some investors would rather store their bullion at their house. Physical gold/silver is usually weighed in grams or in troy ounces and have their purity stamped on them most of them being .999 pure, but can differ from mint to mint. Some mints are even .9999 fine. You can also purchase some bars that have an Assay, which is a bar that has a serial number on a card or sticker that is sealed and cannot be removed with the metal. The card or sticker proves that it meets all standards and its authenticity. These types of pieces will carry a higher premium.

The bullion exchange sets the prices of gold/silver and the price changes with supply and demand. Sometimes price can be changed off of the outlook of the economy. People tend to invest heavily in precious metals when there are global worries. The price that gold/silver are set at is called spot price and can fluctuate. The fluctuation of price can be very volatile. The idea is to buy the bullion as close to spot price as possible. Bullion dealers charge a premium over spot price and that's how they make their money. Sometimes people will turn to online bullion dealers to minimize the premium that is charged. An online business carries less expense, therefore they can charge less. There are some downfalls to online dealers, like shipping and the amount of time until you receive your bullion. There are some benefits of an online dealer, like they usually have more bullion to choose from than a local bullion dealer. If you want to put any bullion into an IRA, they will tell you if it is approved bullion for an IRA and will ship it directly to the IRA Depository. If you want to store your metals in a depository, online is a good option, you just pay the associated fees to the storage depository. I would not recommend an IRA as a beginner investor; the reason being is in case you need the money. With an IRA, you would be penalized if you're not at the minimum age to remove your funds. A lot of older investors will never purchase bullion online due to past experiences during the Great depression in 1933 that forced people to turn in all there gold bars, coins and rounds or they paid very large fines and even served jail time. So, many people like to buy without anyone else having knowledge of their purchases.

Whether you choose a local bullion dealer or an online dealer, it is important that you find a reputable dealer that you can build a business relationship with. The reason for this is, all dealers charge a premium, and when you do business with the same dealer and get to know them, you will get the best deals on the bullion you are buying. Having a good relationship is beneficial when it's time to sell. I like to deal with bullion dealers that deal in high volume atmospheres. Dealing in high volume atmospheres lowers the premium, because they are focused on moving as much bullion as possible, not the premium on each piece. Some local coin shops that don't have a high volume business use a method called the "replacement method." Every time they sell bullion, they will buy what they sold from their wholesaler. So, normally their prices are higher, because they are ordering such a little amount. When you go to a high volume dealer, they may place a $200,000.00 order, so they get a good deal for ordering in bulk, and then can pass that on to you. High volume dealers are also able to give you a better price when you go to sell back your bullion, because the dealers will know it won't take long to sell.

Then you must wonder, how do you know what to buy? We will first focus on the difference between coins, bars and rounds. A coin has a specific face value (tender value) denomination which has precious metal contained in it, they usually have a limited mintage or date range that can be labeled as a collected piece. A bar and a round have no face value (no tender value), they are worth the amount of silver or gold contained within. You can purchase gold/silver bars in many different sizes. For the average investor, the most common size gold bar will start at just a half gram and go from 1 oz. to 10 oz. Much bigger sizes can be bought too, but these are the most common. Bigger gold bars are usually sold for commercial/business uses. The most common gold rounds will come in 1/20 oz., 1/10 oz., 1/4 oz., 1/2 oz., and 1 oz. and can also go up to much larger sizes. Most gold coins will come in the same size as rounds, but most will have a tender value. Many different countries offer gold coins with a tender value, there are one or two countries that make a gold coin with no tender value. The American Gold Eagle is the most common gold coin in the United States which comes in 1/10 oz., 1/4 oz., 1/2 oz., and 1 oz., these all have a different tender value. The most common size of silver bars and rounds are 1 oz., 5 oz., 10 oz. and kilo bars which are 32.15 oz., 50 oz. and 100 oz. bars. There are bigger bars, but they are not commonly sold to investors. Normally, the smaller the coin, round, or bar, the higher the premium you will pay. The American Silver Eagle is the most common silver coin in the United States, and they come in a 1 oz. coin and have a $1.00 face value. Most bars will have the name of the mint/manufacturer and the size bar and the purity of the metal. Some will have real nice designs depending on the manufacturer.

Bar   ***Round***

There is also another type of silver that investors like to purchase, and it is referred to as "junk silver" Or "90 %." Prior to 1965, the United States coins that had silver content like half dollars, quarters, and dimes contained 90% silver and 1965-1970 half dollars had 40% silver. There are certain 1942-1945 nickels commonly referred to as "war nickels" that had 35% silver content. Investors collect these coins just for the silver content. A lot of people like junk silver, there are some coins that were kept in very good shape over the years that people kept to collect. Collectors will get the coins graded by a professional grading service to keep the coins to complete coin sets or sell to collectors to complete their coin collections. This brings in very good money which is based off of the condition of the coin, and the amount of silver content in the specific piece. "Junk silver" is an excellent way to buy silver at a very inexpensive price, (this silver is not pure) it is usually sold by $1.00 face value (if you have 4 quarters from 1964 they are 90% silver and will be .715 oz. of silver). When you're purchasing these 4 quarters, you're not going to be paying the face value of $1.00, you are going to be paying what the current silver value price of .715 oz., plus the premium of what your coin dealer is charging.

90% silver

Many investors also look at something called the gold silver ratio. What this means is, how many ounces of silver can buy 1 ounce of gold. So at the current spot price of gold at$1239.00 divided by the current silver price of $15.37 gives you a ratio of 80:1. Investors normally favor buying silver, when the ratio is a high number, and favor buying gold, when the ratio is a low number. Some investors will try to make money by trading with the ratio, for example, if they buy silver at the ratio of 80:1 and the ratio goes to 50:1 they will sell 50 ounces of silver for an ounce of gold then when the ratio go's back to 80:1, they will sell the gold and end up with 30 ounces of free silver. This is a risky game to play and could be a losing stratagy. You can see from the silver and gold spot price chart, that silver is much more volatile then gold. You can also see from the charts, that throughout history, silver and gold made some very good gains. If you would have bought silver in the early 2000's and sold in 2011 you would have made about 8 and a half times your initial investment. If you would have bought gold in the early 2000's, and sold in 2011 you would have made about 6 and a half times your initial investment. That is some pretty incredible returns.

Courtesy of stockcharts.com

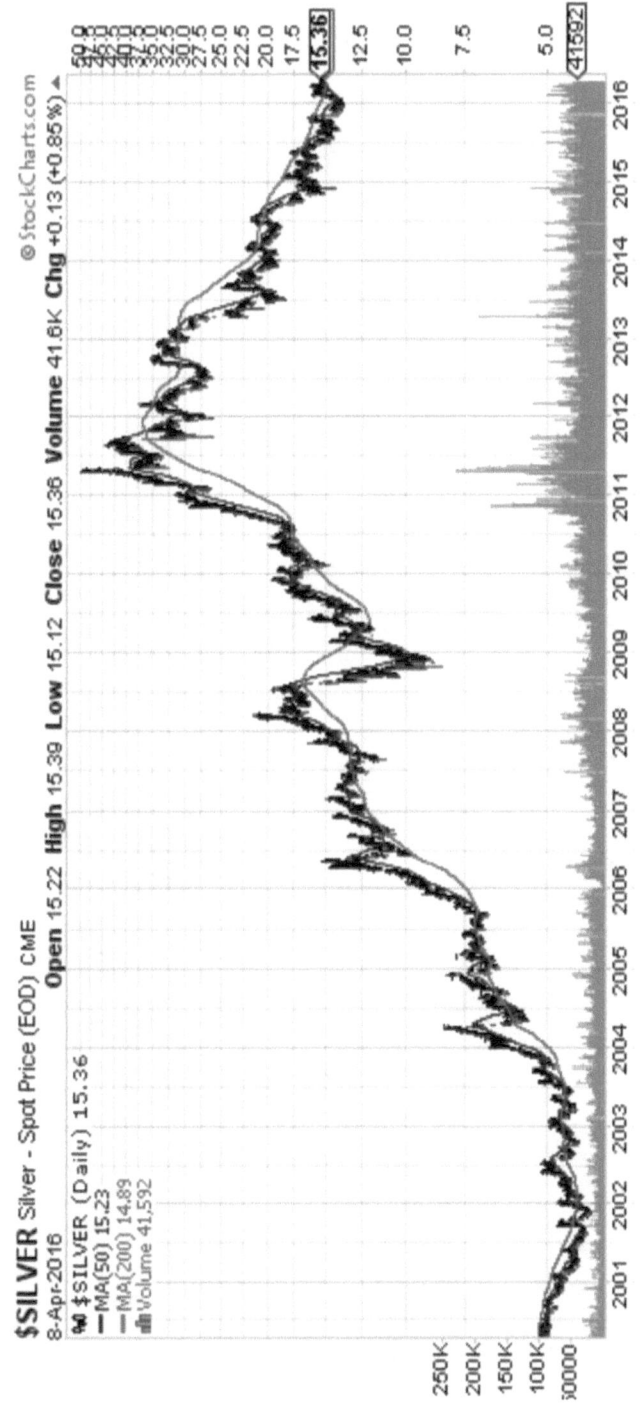

Courtesy of stockcharts.com

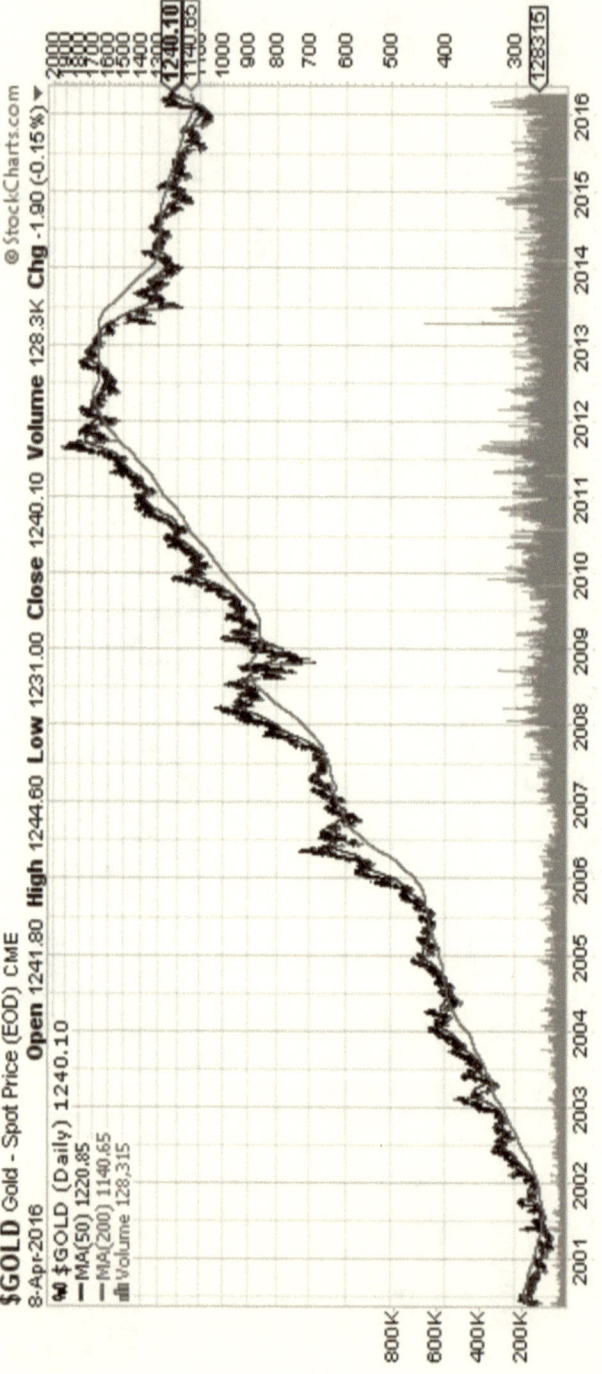

Investors normally stay consistent with purchasing bullion, and when price goes high, maybe wait until the price drops down to return buying. Sometimes buying more as the price drops and less as the price goes up. You should keep a spread sheet to keep track of all your purchases, so you can keep track of how much you have spent. Keeping an average per ounce purchased, so if you decide to sell your bullion, you know how much you need to make, so you're not selling at a loss. Keeping track and using an average is called dollar cost averaging.

The question I always get is... "What bullion should I buy to start?" There is no race on buying precious metals, this can be a life time experience. This is the nice part about small bars and rounds; they are affordable, you may choose to buy a small amount at a time, if you like. Just buying a little at a time is a great strategy maybe biweekly or monthly. I would start out buying a silver bar or two, then the next month buy a silver coin, then the next month buy a small gold coin or some 90% silver. Depending on how much you have to spend will help you budget for your bullion buying.

American Gold Eagle

If you are buying the physical bullion, most investors will store their bullion in tubes. You can usually get tubes from your coin dealer for a very cheap price. Normally 20 ounces of silver or gold usually fit in a tube. So if you buy a tube, you're going to be buying 20 ounces. Just think, if you bought just one ounce of silver a week, you would have a few pounds of silver in a year. A good friend of the family Neil told me when I started out... "Don't put all your eggs in one basket", so I would try to buy a wide range of bullion. Some mints do hold a premium on their bullion over others. Mints that have been in business for years and years have a proven product that people trust and love and will pay the few extra cents to have the name. Buying pieces from different mints will help you stay diverse.

American Silver Eagle

There are coins called proof coins which have the nicest appearance and shine to them and usually have a very hefty premium. I don't recommend these for investing; these are usually bought by collectors and have a limited mintage. These types of coins are usually stored in nice display holders for people to look at. Proof coins will have a deeper detail, due to that they are double struck, compared to the single strike that a normal coin has. Some people will also refer to these as numismatic coins.

Reverse of Morgan Dollar

In summary, what is great is that your investments turn to extra money that you could use towards emergency funds. Precious metals can be turned into cash very quickly. I like to refer to it as an insurance policy. If you can keep the precious metals for long periods, it's a great investment and a great hedge against inflation. There are many different ways to obtain exposure to precious metals. You will have to choose what way works best for you, physical bullion has the lowest risk. Normally when the economy is doing good, metals are low in price, and when the Economy is not doing well, metals soar. Investing in bullion can be fun and rewarding. Sit back, save your 20% and stack your metals and savor the appreciation that these precious metals bring to your savings portfolio.

Stock Market Portfolio

THE NEXT PART OF your investment portfolio should be made up of investing 20% in the stock market. There are several ways to invest, such as stocks, bonds, Exchange traded funds (ETF), mutual funds and 401k plans. I'm going to break these all down for you, and help you understand these different options and decide what benefits you the most.

Many people are nervous about investing money in the stock market; people hear stories about the worst times in history such as the great depression in the 1930's. Many companies went under and people wonder, if this can happen again. This was indeed a horrible time in history, and many people lost their jobs, lifetimes of savings and the homes they lived in. At this time in history, the stock market was doing so good, people were putting all the money they had in the market. Then the most unpredictable happened, it all came crashing down. Putting all your money into stocks is not the best idea, because there will always be ups and downs in the market. This is why I came up with the 60/20/20 split, So you are more diversified and to help you from losing all your hard earned money, if the market does go into a down trend. There is no fool proof method, and there will be times that you think "why did I pick that stock", what was I thinking? There will be times you say "I wish I would have bought more of that stock, it is doing so great". You need to learn when the right time is to take your profits, and the right time to cut your losses, before they become bigger losses. I'm going to explain some of the techniques and indicators I use to pick stocks and the basics of a starting stock investor. Before you can decide what aspect you want to invest in, you have to know some of the basic investment opportunities.

Stocks: When you are taking your money and investing in a company that you believe is a good company that is growing and are doing business right, you then own a portion of a company and are considered a shareholder. You can buy stocks on the stock Exchange. Stocks are more risky then other investments, but have provided better returns than most other investments over a longer period of time.

Bonds: are when a borrower, such as a government, needs a loan possibly to finance a project. For example, if the bond that you buy is a $500 bond, you purchase that bond from the stock exchange. Then you don't get your $500 back until the maturity of the bond. If this is a 5 year bond, you have to wait 5 years to get your original investment back. Since you purchased the bond, the borrower will give you an interest payment every year until the maturity of bond is done. This interest payment is called the coupon rate. If your coupon rate is 3% you would receive $15 dollars a year in interest on your $500 investment. The higher the coupon rate, normally the higher the risk the bond is. It is possible for the borrower to default on a bond and you lose your original investment.

Mutual Funds: are when you have a group of stocks or a group of bonds or a mixture of both grouped together. Instead of just owning a company stock, a mutual fund will buy a group of stocks and you get a fraction of each stock in the fund, this way you will be more diverse. Bonds can be mixed into the fund, as well to lessen the risk involved. There are fees that you pay to have a mutual fund managed and bought and sold. You have to be cautious of these fees, sometimes they outweigh the profit you will make. Most funds need a set amount of money to buy into the fund. Mutual funds are valued at the close of the stock market each day.

Exchanged Traded Funds (ETF): are very similar to mutual funds, they buy a group of stocks and can follow an index, except ETF's trade just like a stock does on the stock exchange. The price will fluctuate throughout the day and will be bought and sold all day. The fees are normally cheaper than a mutual fund and also are easier to buy and sell than a mutual fund.

401K and 403B: plans are very similar, they both invest money into the stock market, and a lot of the plans are set up like mutual funds where you get a group of stocks and bonds. 401k plans are for companies that make a profit; 403B plans are for businesses that are tax exempt or nonprofit. We will talk about the 401k plan. Some employers will offer this plan, and how it works is, you decide how much money you will contribute into the plan. The money will be deducted right out of your paycheck before taxes, so you get a tax break. Some companies will contribute a portion of what you put into the fund, so you get free money. (Everyone loves free money). I always suggest that you put into this fund at least as much as they match. So if they put in up to 3% of what you put in, then you need to try to contribute 3%. The only downfall of a 401k plan is the limited stocks that you're exposed to, some plans are better than others. This type of plan is a retirement plan for this generation. The days of pension plans are just about gone, so to retire these days, this is the plan you will have to depend on. If you're not yet at the point to start putting money into a 401K or 403B plan, take your time And when you're ahead of the game, start by putting the minimum that your employer allows into the account.

There are some terms and language for a starting investor that should be mentioned before diving into the basic investments. You will often hear people say, we are in a <u>bull market.</u> This means that they feel the market is in an upward trend (stock market as a whole is doing well). Then you will hear people say, we are in a <u>bear market.</u> This means that the market is in a downward trend (stock market as a whole is not doing as good as it once was). People often ask "what is the difference between a <u>trader</u> and an <u>investor</u>"? A trader will hold a stock for a short period of time, seconds, minutes, days to weeks maybe a month or two, depending on what kind of trader can hold a position longer. A typical trader likes to buy and sell often. An investor will hold a stock for a longer period of time, usually a year or more and normally holds their positions through the ups and downs in the market. What confused me, when I started into stocks, is when someone says they are long or short in a position. When you are long in a stock means you are buying a stock when the price is low and want it to go higher in price. Most of the time, this is done by an investor like you and I. A short position is when you buy a stock at the high end of a price range and are expecting it to go down in price. This is mostly done by traders, and you have to have a special stock account setup to be in short positions. Shorting is for more advanced investors, so we will be focused on long positions and investing as we go through this section.

Another term that confused me when I started was T+3, which means the day you buy your stock it will be 3 more days until the trade settles and you actually own the stock. The problem with this is, you could actually sell your shares before you own them. As long as you have the cash in your stock account to cover your transaction, you should never run into any problems. If you don't have the money in your account, it is considered free riding, and you can get into some trouble with the brokerage house. The broker house I use has built in protection; you can't buy without sufficient funds. This makes it very hard to run into free riding. I wanted to mention this, because all brokerage houses are not the same, so it will depend on what company you choose.

One thing to be certain of is, no one can predict the future of a company, and when you're buying shares of a company, anything could happen. Sometimes even the companies don't see a problem coming, such as a recall of a vehicle that hurts the sales of that particular brand. People then may sell shares, because the profit of the company is down, and that could hurt the share price. Another incident that could happen is a food borne illness in a restaurant business, because no one is eating at their establishment. The company loses money and investors see that, and sell their shares. Selling the shares causes the price to go down. A lot of investors try to have a stock and bond mixed portfolio to help lessen the risk. The more bond exposure generally lessens the risk of your portfolio, but may not make as good as gains as a stock heavy portfolio. So, you have to find the right ratio for you to determine what is best for you. A basic ratio a lot of investors use is an 80% stock and 20% bond setup. I would say, the younger you are the less bond exposure you need. As you start getting older, maybe add some extra bond exposure for the added protection. If you're 25 years old, you're much more likely to make up for losses over the years, so you can afford to have more risk. If you're 50, you will have much less time to make up your losses. That's why the older you get, the less risk you want to be exposed to.

The first step is setting up a stock account to be able to buy and sell stocks. There are a few different types of accounts to choose from. As a starting investor, you would choose a cash account. A margin account is another very common account used by investors; this is used to short stocks and buys on borrowed money. When setting up a stock account, it is wise to find out how much money you need to open the account. Some require a lot of money, and some do not. You then find out how much they charge you for each stock trade you make.

Some people choose to make all trades online electronically on their own. This is more common than in the past, when you had to call a broker to make your transactions. Some people use a full broker service, and they assist you with your buying. This comes with a price, so remember, the less you have to pay in fees, the more profit you get to keep. And when you have a full broker service, you will pay much more in fees. Most stock accounts charge a set price for as many shares you want to buy, and then a set price for as many you want to sell.

I would recommend letting your stock account build up money, before you actually make your first investment. The reason for this is, if you have $50.00 in your account, and you want to buy a $10.00 stock, if your trade fee is $10.00, that means you can only buy 4 shares. The share price has to go up $2.50 each just to be even. Then, if you would want to sell your shares, you have to be able to cover your seller fee. To further explain, investing with a little amount of money can end up costing you more money. I would recommend about a $500.00 minimum before you start investing. You can deposit your money in your stock account, watch the market and get familiar with the companies you like until you get to that $500.00 dollars. I really like having 5 stocks in separate industries in my portfolio so you can be diverse. If you're unable to afford 5 separate stocks, then an ETF or a mutual fund is probably a better option to start.

When you get to that $500.00, if you say "I don't have the time to watch the market all the time" or "the stocks I like are very expensive", then you could invest in a mutual fund or invest your money into an exchange traded fund (ETF). I personally like ETF's because they trade like a stock and is made up of several stocks, that way you have a wide range of the market in different sectors and funds. Some ETF's can be focused in things like oil, silver, gold, bonds, as well as, the traditional stocks. A lot of people like to find ETF's that track the Standard &Poor 500 (S&P 500) and also the Russell 2000. The S&P are made up of 500 U.S. Large Cap companies and the Russell 2000 are made up of 2000 small cap companies. These indexes are made up of some of the top companies. When you buy an ETF that follow an index, you will get several of the top companies in the index, which will follow the market return as a whole. Investors will compare quarterly or yearly returns of their stocks to the S&P, and most feel they are doing well, if they are beating the return of the S&P.

If you are still thinking that you want to find and pick your own stocks, then I will give you some insight of the things I watch and look at when buying into the company. I like to make a watch list of stocks I may consider buying. I look at the 52 week range where this stock has been. If it is currently at the 52 week high then I wait and see, if it will fall in price before I purchase. There is a new high list that comes out daily, when companies make this list it usually isn't by accident. The companies on this list are most likely doing things right, although there is room for down side action that could make a buying opportunity for you to benefit from. I also look at the price range for 20 years, 10 years and 5 years. If the stock has been falling for the last 20 years and never going up, it will give you a good indication of where it is headed in the future.

A question I ask myself when I pick a stock, Is "if we go into a recession, how bad will this stock be affected?" I feel that needs, such as food and things of that nature, will do well, even in the down times of the market. I will always have one or two of these safe stocks built into my portfolio. Support and resistance are terms to describe a trading range over a time period. When someone says it may break through its support level means a stock is near the bottom of its current trading range, and when it goes below that, that is breaking through its support level. Resistance is the opposite trading range. When the price is at the top of its trading range, and when it continues through that range, it is breaking through the resistance level. When it breaks through that level, usually it will continue in that direction. Most investors try to jump in as it breaks through resistance.

Budget Your Way to Comfort

Courtesy of stockcharts.com

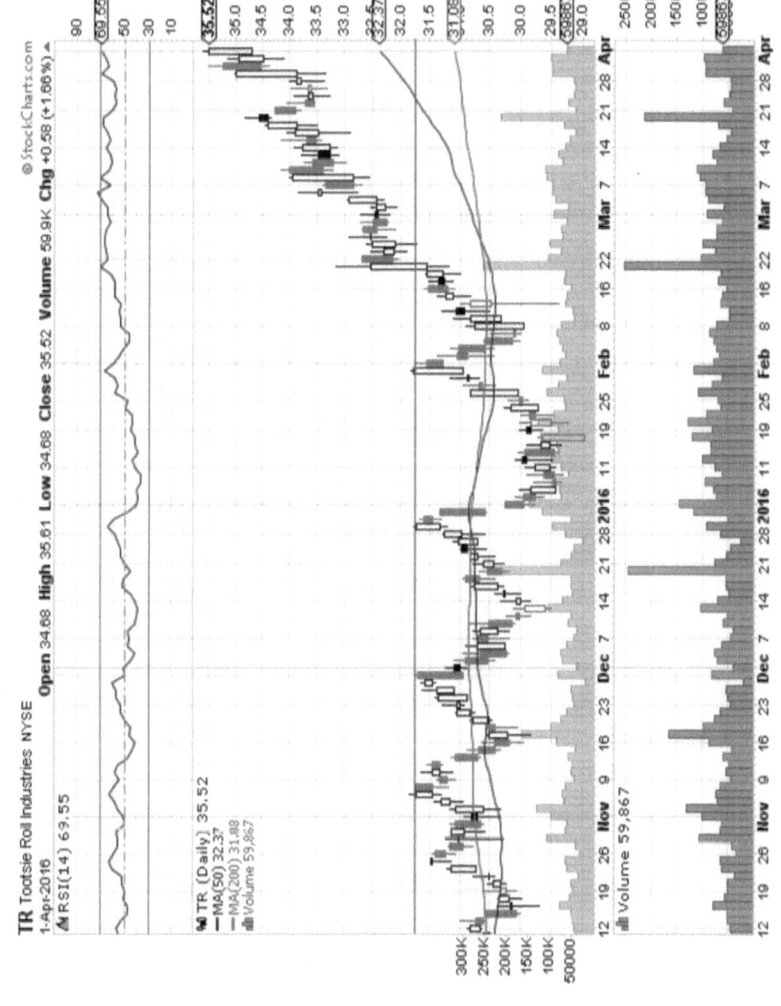

The line going straight across in the chart above is the company's resistance line. This company's stock bounced off of its resistance several times at $31.75, then broke through its resistance level. This company is on a good upside run, and may break through its 52 week high level but, is trading higher than its 50 day moving average and its 200 day moving average. So the price may come back down, as it gets some selling action. When I purchase a stock, I try to purchase below its 50 day moving average. I like to take advantage of when the market as a whole has a bad day. When the prices are down across the board makes a great buying opportunity, especially for proven companies.

Sometimes, stocks that have been in a long downtrend can re-innovate and get the business turned around. I find that the stock market also has sector bull and bear markets. A sector is a group of like businesses such as energy, healthcare, financials, etc.…. they rotate throughout sectors. One whole sector may be in a bear market as another whole sector is in a bull market, you can take advantage of this when investing. For example, if you're looking at a pharmaceutical stock, and a big pharmaceutical company just claimed bankruptcy, this may drive down the whole sector, and this is a buying opportunity for a stock that has a good solid company in that sector.

I like to look at the graphs for companies from different time periods. This is my favorite part of stocks, analyzing charts to try to predict what price the company is going to be at, before it happens. Some fund managers will specialize in analyzing charts, they call this technical analysis. Sometimes they can make moves on stocks, without looking at the facts of the company's income or balance sheet just by looking at the charts. Then some fund managers like to buy and sell off the facts of the income and balance sheet. I like to use the income statement and balance sheet combined with the charts before making a move. I will show you a basic setup of a chart that I look at to see where I think the stock is headed.

Courtesy of stockcharts.com

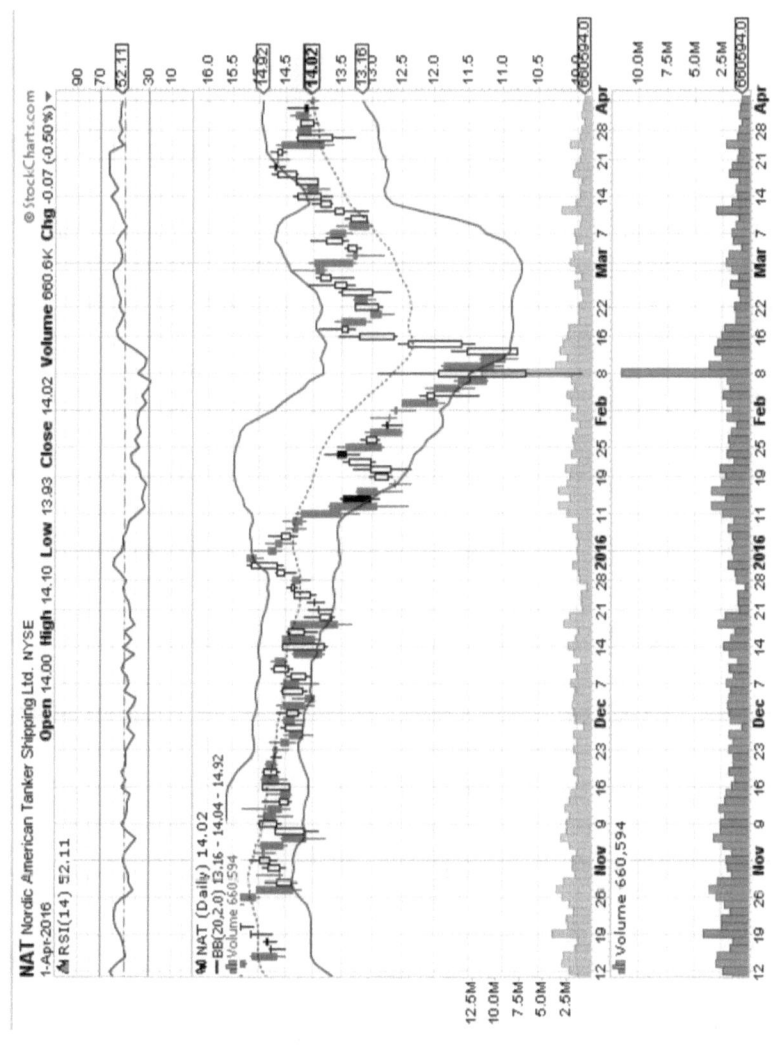

I set my graph up as a candle stick chart, most are set up as a line graph as default. You want to change that to a candle stick chart, and this will show you a lot more information. A single candle stick can tell you a lot about the day. The middle part of the candle is called the Body. If the candle is empty means that the stock went up in price for the day, more than it opened at. If the candle is solid means that the stock went down in price for the day, more than where it opened at. The line coming out of the top of the candle is called the wick. This line indicates the highest point the stock went that day. The line coming out of the bottom of the body is the tail. This line indicates the lowest point the stock went that day. Then you want it set up with something called Bollinger bands. When looking at a Bollinger band graph, the middle line is a trending average usually 14-21 days, then the lines above and below are the general trading ranges that it has been in. (There is a formula used to figure out top and bottom bands).

When the stock drops below the bottom line, this normally indicates an oversold condition. When the stock is above the top line, normally indicates an overbought stock. I wait for a fall in price to go to the bottom Bollinger band, until I buy the stock I am looking at. This has to be used with other techniques not by itself. The Relative Strength Indicator (RSI) is an indicator I use. When this number drops below 30 on the RSI chart, it means it is oversold and may be a buying opportunity. When this number is over 70 means that it is overbought, and may be a good time to take a portion of your profits and run.

I use volume to see if there is a lot of activity. The big spike on the graph above indicates a big purchase when the RSI is very low. I suspect the company bought some of its own stock at a very cheap price, or a big institution bought a big stake in the company at a low price. This can be an indicator the stock price is going to start going the other direction. Same goes if the price is real high, and you see a big volume sell off indicates that the stock may go into a down trend. This will show you a lot of information on the stock price volatility of the stock you're looking at. Although these charts prove right most of the time, there are times when traders can make decisions and these charts lead them in the wrong direction. There are so many different graphs and indicators that you can use for tools to find great companies. There are actually so many, I could write another full book on analyzing charts and indicators.

When I start to research the companies on my watch list, I look at the profit margin of the company and who the CEO is that is running the company. You will hear of a stock company's CEO will resign, and the company will name a new CEO, which makes the stock price go up. The increase in price is because a great CEO can make an average company make huge strides. A bad CEO can turn a good company into a downward spiral. If a stock has been in a downward trend and they get a new CEO, there's a possibility that they could get the stock price turning in the other direction. So I learn as much as possible about the CEO. The CEO can have a direct impact on your hard earned money.

I like to invest in companies that are making a profit. They can have increased revenue, which sounds good, but if they're not making a profit with their increased revenue, then they are taking a loss when selling their product. Another term you will hear people throw around is price to earnings ratio or P/E ratio. Meaning the price you're paying for the stock compared to what the company is earning. Comparing a same sector businesses P/E ratio is a good way to tell, if you're getting the stock you're watching at a cheap price. If you hear someone say that they think a $1000 stock is cheap, they don't mean it doesn't cost a lot of money, they mean the P/E ratio is cheap compared to others in the sector or compared to where the P/E ratio previously was for that stock. Some investors will step up the risk by investing in companies with negative P/E ratios. This is a huge risk and can bring huge gains but, can also bring huge losses.

There is something called an IPO. This stands for Initial Public Offering, when a company is going to be sold on the public stock market, and sometimes you can get shares of the company at an affordable price. The scary part is there is very little research you can do on a company that was private and now going public, so this kind of investment is very risky. So usually when I am looking at an IPO, I look at the banks helping underwrite the deal, and research what other deals that bank has done. If they are reputable named banks making the deal happen, most likely the company will do well. People have made millions investing in new startup companies, but there is extreme risk.

I like to find stocks that pay a good dividend yield, this is a portion of the profit that the company makes, and they give it back to the shareholders. Most companies will allow you to reinvest your dividend back into the company and can create very nice gains. Every time you reinvest, you will then get paid dividends on the reinvested portion. If your reinvested portion isn't enough to create a full share, you will then receive partial shares. If you would rather not reinvest the money back into the company, you can take the dividend amount. Some will send you a check and others will deposit the dividend right into your stock account.

Sometimes you can find a stock that does a stock split, and you can get into a stock at an affordable price.

Companies can do a stock split several ways, but a common stock split is a 2:1 stock split. This means the current shareholder will get double the amount of shares they own after the split, but at half of the current price. If the shares were $50 after the split, they would be $25, but the shareholders would own twice as many as they previously did. The shareholders total value didn't change. This type of split helps lower the share price, makes it more affordable and increases buying, in turn the shares increase in value.

Before you decide to buy the stock you want, do as much research on the stock as possible. News is another thing you have to be always listening to. News of a stock in the same sector as your stock can make your stock go down, and the company that you own is doing great. I read news articles daily, to keep up on anything that can change my stock prices. One way to know a little more about how the company is doing is listening to conference calls and earning reports. This will tell you if they have future plans, if they are making money, or how they plan on spending money. Usually before and after an earnings report, analysts will give ratings of what they think about the company. I take analysts very lightly, just because you don't know who is paying them, and what they are saying is 100% factual. Take into account what they are saying, but don't buy a stock just because an analysts say's they think it's a great stock. Now if you have done your research, and you are watching a stock, and it had a great earnings report and analysts say to buy and everything looks good to you, that is a different story.

I would also advise against buying a stock just because a big name investor bought a stock. I've done this and lost greatly. They are in a different world of investing and have a lot more money than the average investor to get a better deal. This can be a very costly mistake, that I don't want you to make. When you do find the stock you feel is a winner, you will have to put in an order to buy the stock you are looking at. There are several ways to buy and sell your stocks. When you go to place your order, to buy or to sell, you will enter what stock you want and how many shares you want. One way is a <u>market order.</u> This will buy or sell the stock at the going market price of the stock. The downfall is, you could end up paying a lot more or selling for much less than you wanted. The other way is a <u>limit order.</u> This is when you enter a predetermined price and when it gets to that price or under, it will buy the stock. If you use this to sell, it will sell your shares after you get above that price (this is what I personally like to use). The downfall is, if it never gets to the inputted price, it will not buy or sell the shares for you. These seem to be the most common orders, but there are several other ways to do this as well. A <u>Stop-Limit</u> <u>order</u> works much like a limit order, except you set an activation price, and then the stock will stop at that price and become a limit order.

I have covered the most common of the orders you will see as a starting investor. There are other orders that I have not mentioned, and they can differ from one broker service to another. So, you can research what orders you're able to execute when you open your own stock account. Most services default orders the will usually be good for the day. Then at the end of the day, your order will be canceled, if it didn't buy or sell. Your order time can be changed to the day, plus an Extension or good until cancelled. Different brokers will charge different prices for these different orders. Make sure you are familiar with the orders, and what fees you're going to pay, before you execute your order.

Over the last few years, the Federal Reserve (FED) had us at a very low interest rate and is trying to slowly increase interest rates. We have been in a low interest rate environment for some years. When the Economy is doing great, the Fed likes to increase interest rates. Most of the time, higher interest rates will make people spend less money, and can make the economy slowdown and trigger a recession. When the Economy does slowdown, the fed likes to reduce interest rates to encourage spending. The Federal Reserve looks at several different factors such as unemployment numbers, housing sales, car sales, and many other numbers and factors to determine how the economy is doing. This can affect how you invest and what sectors you invest in.

As companies grow, they will actually take on different tasks. Maybe when you bought a stock, they may have specialized in making paint, and the next thing you know, they have grown so much, they start to specialize in restaurant equipment. In this case, often a company will do something that is called a spin off or a split. What this means is, the company will actually separate into 2 companies and this type of move can really benefit shareholders. In this example, the paint company would be the main company and the restaurant equipment would be a separate independent company. When a company does a spin off, most of the time the share price will be cut down, because the main company gives part of the value to the new company. If you already have shares in the main company, they will usually give you a certain amount of shares of the new company, based on how many shares that you currently own of the main company. These type off spin offs can really make new revenue for the company, but also nice gains for the shareholders. If you hear a stock may be splitting, it may be a great opportunity to get into the stock. Split ups don't happen overnight. This can be a very long process, so if you're buying on speculation of a company split, and don't have time to leave your money, staying there for a while may not be a great idea. If you have time to wait and let your money sit in a potential spinoff, you may benefit greatly.

When your stocks are making great gains and you're deciding, if you want to take some of your profits, a lot of times investors question themselves. When deciding if I'm going to take my profit is different from stock to stock. If my stock pays a nice dividend, I may wait until I'm at a 50% gain, before I decide to take any of the profit. If my stock has a minimal dividend and it's close to its 52 week high price and the charts are telling me that the stock might start heading back into a down trend, I may take some of the profit out at a 25% gain. Usually when I take my profits of a nice dividend stock, I don't sell my full position. I take out my initial dollar investment and let the rest of the shares run their course. When you use this technique, you have no money on the line to lose, you would be using free money at this point. Never base a decision to buy or sell on emotion. Sometimes you will see your stock start going down very quickly, and your emotions may take over, and you sell quickly than 2 hours later the stock makes a full recovery. So it's a smart idea to have a predetermined price in mind that you would like to sell. This will keep your emotions out of the decision process.

When you buy a stock and it starts going into a down trend, usually emotions take over and investors hold, because they don't want to take a loss. If you plan on holding this stock for the long haul, I would add to my position and lower the price of what you own the stock for. If you really don't know why you bought the stock in the first place, or planned on trading the stock for a quick profit, then cut your losses and put the remaining money into a stock that has some upside potential. This is where becoming a trader or investor is different. If you're investing, just hold out. If you're trading stocks, cut your losses before they turn to bigger losses. You need to have a mindset, before entering a stock, of what your strategy is going to be, when you will buy and when you will sell, or how many years you're going to hold the stock. I always make a predetermined plan with my stocks in my portfolio, before I buy them. If my initial plan is to hold a stock for 15 years, I will not worry about the day to day price movement of the stock and try to add to my position every time it drops down one point or 1 dollar. If you have no idea what stock you want to buy, using a stock screener is a great tool to use. They allow you to input what criteria you're looking for in a stock, such as price, dividend, P/E ratio and many others.

You will pay taxes on your profit that you collect. This is called capital gain taxes. If you hold your stocks longer than a year, you pay a lower tax percent than someone that holds their stocks for a shorter period of time. If you do make some poor decisions and decide to take some losses, you can also claim losses on your taxes as well. If you're not sure of what capital gain taxes you will owe, you should contact a tax professional to determine what will work best for you.

In summary, you're not always going to be right every time. But, there are many different ways to invest in the stock market. After using some of these tools, and doing research before just jumping into a stock, this will give you a better educated decision about a company. Bonds are a great tool to lessen your risk and diversify your portfolio. As you get older, your portfolio makeup should become more conservative and less aggressive. Possibly include more bond exposure and less stock exposure. You should read all you can and research any stock that you're interested in and watch it for a little while before diving in. The CEO of a company can have a great impact on a stock that you like, and dividends can give you an extra boost of income to your portfolio. Splits can help you get into a great company at a discount price. Remember as you enter into the stock market, just relax, stay calm, keep your emotions out of decisions and diversify.

Conclusion

As YOU CLOSE MY book, you should have a basic foundation to stabilize a proper budget, save money and start investing in many different avenues. Starting the investment process can be a nerve racking experience. Before investing in any market situation, you need to make sure you fully understand the market you are investing in. Being a money saver is a trained skill, stocks will have ups and downs, but holding them for long periods of time as an investor can really build great gains. Good things take time; most of the time you will not achieve results overnight. It is very easy to be a spender, the big step is to save that extra money and not spend it. I find that a lot of the time, when people have money, they feel they have to spend it. When investing money, it helps with the feeling that you needed to spend money but you actually still have the money, just not the same way you did. The nice part is, if you do run into a serious situation, stocks and precious metals can be sold to collect the cash.

Saving and investing creates a little nest egg of extra money, in case you encounter financial hardship. Investing your money can work for you and make a nice profit in several different ways. Investing can also turn into a fun hobby that you can enjoy, and share with your friends. I find that surrounding yourself around people that are interested in the same saving habits as you will help you in your quest to be a successful money saver. The people you socialize with will usually have an influence on you. If they like to spend big, you may be influenced to be a spender. Sometimes things will come up and may get you off track of your quest to save. When you are learning to walk and fall down, you don't give up on learning to walk. You have to have the same mindset when a hiccup happens in your financial plans, to keep moving in the right direction. Just keep your portfolio diverse and keep focused on the goals you set for yourself and celebrate your goals when you accomplish them. Buckle down and keep saving and budget your way to comfort!

Glossary

About the Author

Luke Brandt was born and raised in Lancaster, Pennsylvania. He is an up and coming author who became interested in creating budgets and investing, after overcoming some of his own financial obstacles. He has a passion for helping others find financial success and wants to introduce others to the same techniques that he uses.